The

Journey To

Wholeness

by

Dr. Cynthia L. McGill

The Journey To Wholeness
Copyright © 2001 Dr. Cynthia L. McGill

ISBN-0-9714965-0-1

Published By:
Dominion Kingdom Publishers
Post Office Box 11246
Rochester, New York 14611

DEDICATION

No undertaking is accomplished alone. I would like to dedicate this undertaking to:

My family who has supported this work in every way that you can dream. My father, John Tarpley, who has gone to be with the Lord, and who always believed I could do anything. My mother, Doris and my sisters, Jewel, Vanita and Melony - they are my biggest supporters. My husband, Reggie, who is also my Pastor, my lover and my best friend – your love, devotion encouragement and support are the keys that have unlocked the passion in my heart to fulfill my destiny with great power and strength. My encouraging daughters, Maia and Adrienne and granddaughter, Gabrielle – you bring such joy to my life.

My editor, friend and co-worker, Rose Nichols – you helped to make this venture possible. The women of New Life Fellowship - they inspire me daily on my journey to wholeness. And ultimately, to my Lord Jesus Christ, who is **THE** source of all my strength.

TABLE OF CONTENTS

INTRODUCTION:
JOURNEY INSTRUCTIONS

My Dear Sister,

All of us want to be tenderly loved and reaffirmed everyday in every way. However, in reality, the journey called "life" can be the most difficult road to travel. Especially if we have shared the early days of our journey with other travelers known to us as parents, siblings and friends who have neglected, rejected and devalued us.

The other travelers sharing various aspects of our busy lives may not always realize the significant responsibilities they share in filling our life journey with hope and love.

You may now be at a place in your life where the construction, detours and roadblocks you have had to endure on your journey seem to mar your path to personal fulfillment, success and excellence. You may identify with signs like this one...

To you, this sign means that people have been working on "your last nerve" for what seems like forever or distracting you from the sidelines that has caused you to be emotionally and/or physically abused, neglected or just plain devastated. You may even view this sign as a reminder that someone in your life has been controlling you for years, never allowing you to develop into the woman God has destined for you to become.

Isaiah 59:7 states...

"Their feet run to evil, and they make haste to shed innocent blood. Their thoughts are thoughts of iniquity; desolation and destruction are in their paths and highways." (AMP)

During this part of the journey you have been slowed down and/or reduced to believe you have nothing to offer. BUT WAIT! CHECK OUT THIS SIGN!

☞ DEAD END DRIVE
LIVING WHOLE HIGHWAY ☞

IT'S NOT TOO LATE! However, it is up to you. You can back track until you end up at "Dead End Drive" or you can gird up your loins and travel this journey with me toward "Living Whole Highway"! God is not a God of the dead but of the living! God has a better life for you! A life filled with a great connection to Jesus Christ!

Now I am sure you are asking, "How do I get to Living Whole Highway?" Well, in order to complete this trip you need journey instructions. A road map that will help you understand the relationship you can have with God that is filled with love, joy and peace.

You must commit to reading this "manual" and allow the Holy Spirit to bring you to full attention as you travel through every passage. Passage is defined as the act of passing; specifically movement from one place to another; migration, change or progress from one process or condition to another; transition; a journey.

You must also ask the Holy Spirit to fill you with wisdom so you can come to a full realization of who you are and whose you are in the Kingdom of God. *Ask* the Holy Spirit to fill you with wisdom as you take this trip. Proverbs 3:17 states that wisdom's *ways are* ways of pleasantness and all *her paths are* peace.

Bringing wisdom as a travel companion will be of great benefit to you. My hope is that when you are ready to take the exit on to Living Whole Highway you will not only have gained wisdom but also have begun to acquire the benefits of long life, wealth, honor and peace.

Do not travel these passages impaired by doubt or fear. Protect yourself with the whole armor of God so that you are not *"tossed [like ships] to and fro between chance gusts of teaching and wavering with every changing wind of doctrine, [the prey of] the cunning and cleverness of unscrupulous men, [gamblers engaged] in every shifting form of trickery in inventing errors to mislead."* Ephesians 4:14 (AMP) Travel each passage by faith, not by sight.

The first 3 passages (chapters) on this journey are designed to help you fully comprehend and understand the breadth, length, height and depth of the devotion and love God has towards you. We will begin with giving you a special key that must be ignited in order for the journey to begin as well as give you a green light in the discussion about affirmation.

Passages 4 – 6 are cautionary courses that outline the dangers of "grasshopper thinking", deception, self-will, guilt and unforgiveness. This set of cautionary passages ends with the reassurance that God has done it all for you! The last three passages on this journey to wholeness is intended to provide you with a few basic truths that will allow you to "know that you know that you know that you know" you are well connected and whole. These passages of insight and knowledge will prepare you as you safely make the "inner change" on to "Living Whole Highway".

Before we begin, please remember that whether or not you travel this journey to wholeness is solely (and "soul-ly") up to you. What I mean is that in order to make this journey your emotions, mind and will have got to be ready and willing to go. Whether or not you take this trip is wholly up to you.

God has commissioned me to write this "manual" and relate this journey experience to you for a purpose. The purpose is to share a life changing experience with you. This manual is a gift to you from God. Will you make the right decision? Will you look ahead to "Living Whole Highway" and go on this journey to wholeness?

Yes!?! Well then, let's go! Before we begin, please sit comfortably with both hands on this book. Remember to put on the full armor of God because you cannot afford to let your attention wander from what you are about to experience. As it states in the Amplified translation of Hebrews 12:2...

"Looking away [from all that will distract] to Jesus, Who is the Leader and the Source of our faith [giving the first incentive for our belief] and is also its Finisher [bringing it to maturity and perfection]."

The last journey instruction is this... The journey to wholeness is an arduous one indeed. It is a journey that takes an intimate look forward towards excellence, fulfillment, success and wholeness. As we embark upon this journey, feel free to chart your own "personal pavement marks" as you complete the exercises prescribed throughout the book.

There are certainly many lanes and routes one could take. This particular journey manual describes one jaunt. Follow along, if you dare, and be honest with yourself, as you uncover hidden treasures within yourself. I do believe that with the comfort, guidance and power of the Holy Spirit, Jesus will shine alight on your past path and at the same time help you deal with the blinding effects on you presently so that you can see yourself whole.

From My Heart to Yours,

Dr. Cynthia L. McGill

Passage One

Before We Start...
Let's Get Real

Before we begin this journey we must take a deep introspective look at ourselves so that each passageway we encounter can be faced with inner truth. In Psalm 51:6 it states,

"Behold, You desire truth in the inner being; make me therefore to know wisdom in my inmost heart."

In order to desire truth in the inner being you must possess a very important key. One of the definitions of a key is "something regarded as a key in opening or closing a way, revealing or concealing; an instrument, usually of metal, for moving the bolt of a lock and thus locking or unlocking something". Without this key you will not be able to begin your journey to wholeness.

This key is called the "Get Real" key. Repeat this: "Lord, I want to get real". Matthew 7:3-5 (AMP) says:

"Why do you stare from without at the very small particle that is in your brother's eye but do not become aware of and consider the beam of timber that is in your own eye? Or how can you say to your brother, Let me get the tiny particle out of your eye, when there is the beam of timber in your own eye? You hypocrite, first get the beam of timber out of your own eye, and then you will see clearly to take the tiny particle out of your brother's eye."

In order to "get real" with yourself you must come clean from pretending and recognize your struggles. If you do not, you will try to begin your trip with a very dangerous key that may look

 like it will get you where you want to go but it will not. It is shaped like a skeleton key and it is called "HYPOCRISY".

This key is the exact opposite of the "Get Real" key. Webster defines hypocrisy as:

❖ Acting a part
❖ Pretending
❖ Pretending to be what one is not

Do you want to "Get Real" or be a "wannabe" trying to pass as a whole woman? Women are taught to pretend. As little girls we were taught to bat our eyes and cry so our dads, moms or grandparents would let us have our way. Some married women pretend to have a headache. Some single women pretend either all men like them or all men hate them. Some Christian women pretend they are so spiritual. We pretend to God, to others and to ourselves. Hypocrisy is a dangerous key to try to use on this road. It's delusional; it's insidious; it keeps us from being real before God, others and ourselves.

Some of us would rather live a life of hypocrisy. We want to pretend we have it altogether; we want to pretend we are whole and complete and self-assured. If we are not careful, the hypocrisy key will only turn the engine on to delusional thinking. I once knew a woman who was widowed at an early age and left to raise several small children by herself. She would tell everyone what a rich life she had when her husband was alive. She would constantly talk about the money, homes and expensive vacations they had when he was alive. I later learned none of what she had said was true. Why was she "pretending"? I am not a psychologist and therefore, I will not set forth my own assertions. However, I can look at the scriptures for guidance on her delusional state and tell you that not being real with yourself is delusional and dangerous. Ephesians 4:22-24 in the Amplified states,

"Strip yourselves of your former nature [put off and discard your old unrenewed self] which characterized your previous manner of life and becomes corrupt through lusts and desires that spring from delusion; And be constantly renewed in the spirit of your mind [having a fresh mental and spiritual attitude], And put on the new nature (the regenerate self) created in God's image, [Godlike] in true righteousness and holiness".

We must use the "Get Real" key and come to understand ourselves and desire truth in the inner being.

I love the story of the Prodigal son. He eventually came to understand that he had to use the "Get Real" key. The Prodigal son "came to himself". He recognized that he had been silly to run away from home; that he had been hurting himself, that he had been hurting others. <u>He recognized his sin.</u> He knew he would go home, that he could meet his father again and that his father would forgive him.

The Prodigal son is a parable that exemplifies the love of God toward us. We turn our backs on God; we leave "home" and often lead life on the wild side, then are afraid to go "home". We often are afraid to "come to ourselves" and ask God to forgive us and take us back. But, He is always there with open arms waiting to welcome us "home" – back in fellowship with Him.

Today, many women struggle with emotional pain that is deeply rooted in the past. If we look in the rearview mirror at our past we may see how unresolved pain manifests itself in our over-extended lifestyles. We:

❖ **Over-eat**   ❖ **Over-work**

❖ **Over-spend**   ❖ **Over-commit**

❖ **Over-obsess**   ❖ **Over-spiritualize**

We need to focus on the course before us in order to bring balance into our lives. Balance comes only after being freed from emotional baggage and pain.

Now that we have gotten started by using the "Get Real" key to ignite our body, soul and spirit, let's get rid of as much baggage before we truly begin the journey. In what areas of your life do you struggle the most and have the heaviest baggage?

- ❏ Over-eating
- ❏ Over-spending
- ❏ Sexual promiscuity
- ❏ Envy
- ❏ Insecurity
- ❏ Fear of…
- ❏ Controlling nature ("I need to control others")
- ❏ Over-work
- ❏ Over-spiritualize
- ❏ Over-cleanliness (the house, etc.)

GET REAL

Just because you may have a successful career, a beautiful home, and/or a little bit of money in the bank, does not guarantee instant healing from deep emotional scars and pain.

I want you to take a moment and look outside your window at the beautiful, giant redwood tree. If you study redwood trees you will find that they are strong survivors. If you look at a cross section of a giant, beautiful redwood tree that has been cut, you will see numerous rings that reveal the history of that tree. Due to its growth rings and its many centuries of life, a redwood can provide a sort of map of history. A cross section of a fallen tree shows the major points in its history. The rings are defined as "a series of dark and light concentric markings with a tree's trunk that indicate the annual growth of the tree".

You are like the great, beautiful redwood tree. You have a series of dark and light concentric markings. There are scars or "rings" of painful hurts from your past. Perhaps in your redwood tree of life there is the scar of an alcoholic father who was abu-

17

sive. Conceivably there is the scar of an abortion that took place at the age of fifteen. The scar of a mother who made you feel that nothing you did was ever good enough. The "ring" left from an abusive husband. Those memories, scars, "rings" affect our concepts, feelings and relationships. They affect the way we look at life, others and ourselves.

What are the inner rings of your past?

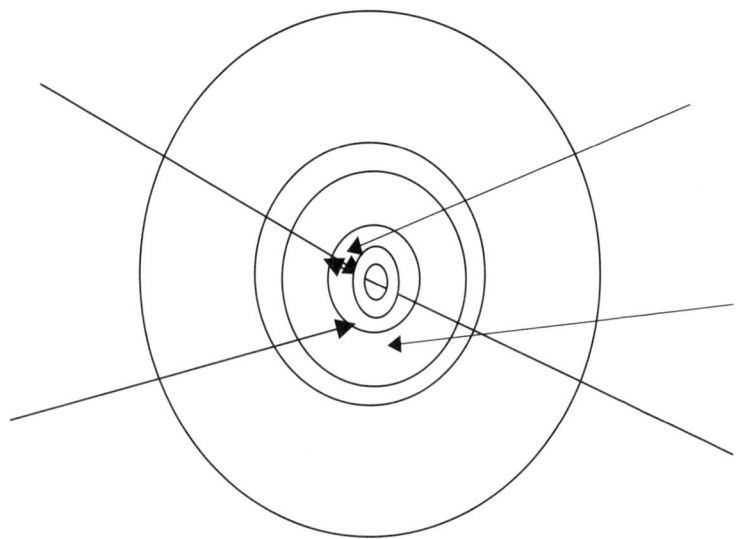

These emotional scars are rings that create a deep sense of unworthiness, inferiority, or a sense that you must be perfect at all times and at all costs. You must be healed so that you can keep growing like the redwood tree. Remember I stated that redwood trees are strong survivors? Well, the principle reason that virgin coast redwoods have lived for 2,000 years or more is that only the most radical assaults can kill them. You, like the redwood tree have hope! Read Habakkuk 3:17-19 in the Amplified:

Though the fig tree does not blossom and there is no fruit on the vines, [though] the product of the olive fails and the fields yield no food, though the flock is cut off from the fold and there are no cattle in the stalls, Yet I will rejoice in the Lord; I will exult in the [victorious] God of my salvation! The Lord God is my Strength, my personal bravery, and my invincible army; He makes my feet like hinds feet and will make me to walk [not to stand still in terror, but to walk] and make [spiritual] progress upon my high places [of trouble, suffering, or responsibility]!

Your unanswered questions about your past may lead to more questions, which could lead to spirit destroying doubt. Up until now you may have chosen to live with your doubts, trying to ignore them and trying even still to move on with life. You may even be at the point of cynicism and have a hard heart.

However, there are those who will reject the destroying doubt and cynicism and continue on their journey. You have hope. Hope means going beyond our unpleasant experiences to the joy of wholeness. Habakkuk's feelings were not controlled by the events around him but by faith in God's ability to give him strength. Just like Habakkuk your feelings do not have to be controlled by your past because God gives strength! Take your eyes off of difficulties and look to God. Take your "Get Real" key and unlock your life in order to ignite the fire within. This key will help you keep on task and will definitely increase the speed of your journey. The "Get Real" key will make your journey much easier and will give you the surefooted confidence to continue.

Habakkuk boldly and confidently took his complaints directly to God and God answered. As you continue to the next passage listen for God's answers and rejoice that the Holy Spirit is at work in your life. As you travel this journey live in the strength of His Spirit, confident in the ultimate victory. Be assured that He is God and He will lead you to the "Living Whole" Highway.

Passage Two

The Journey Begins

Now that we have used the "Get Real" key and have ignited our engines, let us get started on our journey. I do not know about you but every time I get ready to go on a journey, I over pack. My husband smiles and asks, "And how long are we staying?" The question, of course, is poking fun at me and highlighting the fact that I do not need four suitcases for a weekend trip!

Oftentimes on life's journey, we simply carry around too much baggage. Some of the baggage does not even belong to us!

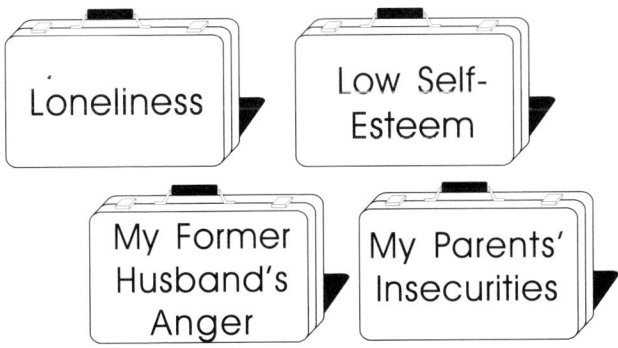

I know that how our parents and other adults treated us growing up shapes and molds our personalities and images of ourselves. Growing up in a loving, nurturing environment creates a secure, confident child. As we know, if the environment in which we were raised was negative and if we felt rejected and unloved, more often than not, we grow up struggling to regain positive self-esteem and self-worth. We will talk more about this when we enter Passage Three, however, let us begin the journey by accepting this important life-changing TRUTH:

**MY PAST AND
MY BACKGROUND
DO NOT DEFINE
MY PRESENT OR
MY FUTURE**

This is a road sign we will need to acknowledge in order to overcome past obstacles in the road. Repeat the road sign words out loud. Romans 12:2 in the Amplified Bible says:

Do not be conformed to this world (this age), [fashioned after and adapted to its external, superficial customs], but be transformed (changed) by the [entire] renewal of your mind [by its new ideals and its new attitude], so that you may prove [for yourselves] what is the good and acceptable and perfect will of God, even the thing which is good and acceptable and perfect [in His sight for you].

This is probably the most difficult "TRUTH" or "road sign" to acknowledge and accept along life's journey. We cannot allow our past to define us. We must allow God's Word (the "TRUTH") to define who we are and who we are becoming. We can only do this by renewing our mind in the Word of God. If we do not embrace this truth and believe it, by faith, we will be detoured for years.

I have counseled dozens of women who have so much potential and are so gifted but do not see themselves that way. I have also counseled absolutely beautiful women (beautiful inside and out!) who think they are ugly and undesirable! These women are looking at themselves through the eyes of unloving,

PEOPLE CAN ONLY TREAT YOU AS GOOD AS THEY FEEL ABOUT THEMSELVES

unsupportive people from their past who carried around their own baggage.

Here is another "TRUTH" and road sign to accept:

If the people in your past could not support, love or encourage you, it is only because they, themselves, were not loved, supported and encouraged. Now, I am not trying to cast blame upon your parents, grandparents and others. I truly believe they did the best they could with what they knew and how they felt about themselves. The "blame game" is only another roadblock anyway, right? As long as we keep assigning blame to others, we will never move forward on our journey.

Poor self-esteem (negative, condemning feelings about yourself) is baggage that keeps us under condemnation and causes us to be less than God intends. Proper self-esteem is a process of embracing the "TRUTH" that Jesus' work on the cross makes us a brand new creature free from those past roadblocks.

Philippians 3:13 in the Amplified Bible says:

I do not consider, brethren, that I have captured and made it my own [yet]; but one thing I do [it is my one aspiration]: forgetting what lies behind and straining forward to what lies ahead.

Moving forward (which is sometimes a strain, yes indeed) along this journey, you will need to:

Get Beyond Yourself

Grow Beyond Yourself

And

Go 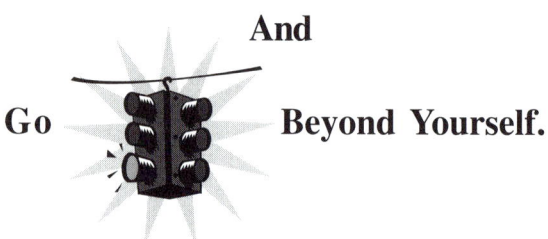 **Beyond Yourself.**

In order to "Get Beyond Yourself", you must <u>choose</u> to renew your mind daily with God's Word. To "Grow Beyond Yourself", it will be necessary to <u>exercise</u> your choice to live in the Spirit of God and walk out God's Word each and every day, one step at a time. The more you walk in the Spirit, the more you choose to have your mind renewed and transformed each day, the more you choose to accept who you are because of Christ, the more you will "Go Beyond Your Past Self" and become all God intended you to be.

Passage Three

Affirmation and Reaffirmation

Let us progress to an examination of the words "affirm" and "reaffirm". The American Heritage Dictionary defines "affirm" and "reaffirm" as follows:

> Affirm = to declare positively or firmly; maintain to be true. To ratify or confirm.
>
> Reaffirm = to affirm or assert again.

Therefore reaffirm also means to again declare positively or firmly; maintain to again be true; to again ratify or confirm. These definitions should lead you to begin to understand that to be affirmed you must declare to yourself positive attributes and qualities as well as hear affirmations again from others traveling this journey with you.

Answer some simple questions for yourself:

1.   Who "affirmed" and "reaffirmed" you as a worthwhile human being as a child?

2.	What values were instilled in you as a child?

3.	Did you feel validated? Special? Belittled? What happened to make you feel this way?

I will always remember a time in 6th grade when I wanted to start a school newspaper. One day I was feeling down because I was trying to write all the articles by hand. I needed a typewriter. I did not even tell my mom that I needed one; she just saw me struggling.

My mother found an old (but good) typewriter and told me, "Honey, you can do it; do not get discouraged. What you need is a typewriter." I pecked those keys one at a time with a smile on my face. And, you know what? I did it! Through the affirmations and support of my mother, I produced a two-page newspaper for my elementary school!

Perhaps you were not affirmed or reaffirmed growing up as a child in the natural growth process. One major responsibility of your parents in raising you was to show forth the compassionate love of God, which is sincere and strong, and to instill in you a positive self-esteem that integrated respect and validation of self. When that does not happen, we can search for years – usually looking in the wrong places – for acceptance, love and validation – for true affirmation that can only come from God.

You may then ask, well where can affirmation of me come from now if I did not receive it earlier in my life? Well, as I stated, affirmation now can come from God the Father. His affirmation of you is throughout the Bible and is both personal and positive. For example, in Jeremiah 31:3 (AMP) it says, "The Lord appeared from of old to me [Israel], saying, Yes, I have loved you with an everlasting love; therefore with loving-kindness have I drawn you and continued My faithfulness to you." This one scripture affirms so much in so many ways. This scripture tells you that God's love for you is personal and attractive (it draws you).

There has **never** been a moment when God has not loved you. Nothing can separate you from God's love once you have repented of your sins. God, through this one affirming statement (and there are thousands more throughout the Bible), reaches toward you with kindness motivated by His deep and everlasting love. He is eager to do the best for you if you will only let Him. This reminder of God's affirming love for you should be a breath of fresh air for you. You may not have been affirmed or reaffirmed as a child, however, now that you have confessed Jesus Christ as the Lord of your life and been born again in the Spirit, God the Father can affirm and reaffirm you again and again through His Word and His intimate fellowship time with you. Now others in the Body of Christ who are filled with His agape love can and should reaffirm you too!

There is an example in John 8:1-11 of a woman who was affirmed by Jesus. The woman mentioned had an adulterous affair (or, affairs) because she **probably did not** feel good about herself. She may have had a poor self-image. The Pharisees brought in the woman who was caught in adultery. Then, the Pharisees and scribes asked Jesus, "Now, what do you say?" They wanted to trap Jesus. If Jesus refused to confirm the death penalty, he could be charged with contradicting the law of God and would himself be liable to condemnation. If, on the other hand, he confirmed the verdict of the Pharisees, he would lose his reputation for compassion.

What did Jesus do? He finally rose and in verse 7 he said, "If anyone of you is without sin, let him be the first to throw a stone at her." In verse 9 it says, "Those who heard." I would also say and those who were convicted by their consciences went "one at a time, the older ones first". Then it was just Jesus and the woman. Jesus asked the woman and He's asking **you** today: "Has no one condemned you?" She said, "No one, sir." Jesus said to the woman and He's saying to you today: "Then neither do I condemn you. Go now and leave your life of sin."

God is telling you today, "Woman, go and sin no more." "Go and lie no more." "Go and gossip no more." "Go and fornicate no more." "Go and be envious no more." God **affirmed** that woman in the Bible. She is now somebody in Christ. You are somebody in Christ.

Let us look at this affirming story on another level. As the accusers of the woman left her one at a time one could say that this is an example of her sins also leaving her one at a time. My dear Sister, God is trying to tell you that no one is accusing you. All of your accusers have left one at a time. They were a distraction to you as you tried to travel the course to wholeness. They surrounded you on every side but you are not crushed. They tried to embarrass and perplex you all about but you are not driven to despair.   All of your accusers have left one at a time. All of your sins, misgivings and weights concerning you are leaving.

You relate to other people based on how you feel about yourself and/or how they made you feel. This is the same theme with the woman caught in adultery. Therefore Jesus had to affirm her. Not only did He forgive her sins but He also affirmed her as a woman.

Jesus is telling you today that no one is left; no one from your past, no one from your present. They are all gone. Why? Due to the fact that they did not affirm or reaffirm you. They are no longer important. It is not important what people from your past have said or are saying about you. Now it is just you and Jesus!

Know that only your Creator can affirm you. Subsequently, people reaffirm what was already spoken. My Creator, Jesus Christ, said that Cynthia is fearfully and wonderfully made (Psalm 139:14) which means I am unique, wonderful and a worthwhile person. God thinks of you constantly in the same way. Therefore, reaffirm yourself as much as your Creator does. Complete the following sentence: "Jesus, my Creator says I am

_____.

Therefore I do not have to wait for a stamp of approval from man to declare that I am beautiful and worthy." This is the first evidence of wholeness because it leads to:

1. An intimate relationship with God,
2. A positive feeling of self-worth/self-esteem,
3. Positive, healthy relationships with others.

If you are willing to believe and show forth evidence of affirmation and reaffirmation then you have safely progressed through this passage and are well on your way to fully comprehending and understanding the breadth, length, height and depth of the devotion and love God has for you. You now have the green light to go forth to the next passages that are cautionary courses that outline some dangers that may be seen or unseen by the naked eye but can be revealed if you are spiritually able and ready. Now sister, Go! And sin no more!

Passage Four

Cautionary Course 1: Grasshopper Thinking

You may not feel it, but you have come a long way on your journey to wholeness. You have the "Get Real Key" which has started you on your way. You have begun the journey and are now showing evidence of a more intimate relationship with God, positive feelings of self worth and endeavoring to have healthy relationships with others. It may even seem like you "have it made" now. You can coast to "Living Whole" highway. Uh-oh! It is that kind of "I have arrived" thinking that can suspend or revoke your privilege to continue on this journey.

I want to share with you now the kinds of thinking that can "arrest" your progress and cause your journey to be violated. If you do not read the road signs carefully while traveling these next few cautionary courses, you will suffer condemnation and/or spiritual violations that could cause you to roll over into a ditch of despair. The Holy Spirit will then have to tow you to God's garage for refuge, which may take some time. After the renewal repairs are done, you will be in better shape to try a second time, but you may have to start back at Passage One.

Keep moving forward, cautiously, on this road that has many curves and twists. Be assured that the Holy Spirit is here with you and will help you at every turn to overcome the bumps and potholes so you can holdfast to that which Christ Jesus has for you. The first cautionary course is "Grasshopper Thinking". As you read, carefully examine your heart to see if you identify yourself as "a persistent violator".

How often in life does God set before us the possible, the good, and the best – but because of our negative mindset, because of a defeatist attitude, we prevent ourselves from becoming whole and receiving all God has for us. Having a preconception of defeat is the very thing that prevented the children of God from entering the Promised Land. In Numbers 13:33b (NIV), "…we seemed like grasshoppers in our own eyes…". The people saw themselves as grasshoppers.

What is going on in Numbers 13? Well, the Lord told Moses to send men to explore and spy out the land of Canaan. The men returned and gave Moses this account in Numbers 13: *We went into the land to which you sent us, and it does flow with milk and honey. Here is its fruit. But the people who live there are powerful, and the cities are fortified and very large. Then Caleb silenced the people before Moses and said, "We should go up and take possession of the land, for we can certainly do it." But the men who had gone up with him said, "We can't attack those people; they are stronger than we are." "…We **_seemed_** like grasshoppers in our own eyes…"*

Let us define the word "seem" (Webster's Dictionary): to appear to be; give the impression of being; to appear in one's own mind. "Grasshopper thinking" has held us captive, bound us up and kept wholeness out of our grasp. Often times we get caught up or hung up on what "seems" to be holding us back from becoming whole. It "seems" we will always feel guilty of some past deed or deeds. We feel as if we can never forgive others or ourselves. It "seems" we are stuck in a revolving door of unforgiveness going round and round; never becoming free. It "seems" as if wholeness is just an illusion and we are sentenced to a life of never quite possessing a positive feeling of self-worth. The "possession of the land" as referred to in verse 30 could easily be the "possession of wholeness". However we, like the men in Numbers 13, do not feel we can possess what is rightfully ours. The only way we will step into wholeness and break from "grasshopper thinking" is to see ourselves as Christ sees us.

How do we learn to stop seeing ourselves as failures, as someone with low self-worth? Or, how do we shed the appearance of seemingly having it altogether when deep down we are feeling insecure, lonely – sometimes, even in the midst of having material wealth? How do I shed this "grasshopper" covering? How do we put-on the "Caleb" covering – the covering of "we can certainly do it" or in the King James Version, "We are well able"?

Let us examine seven principles for beginning to see ourselves as Christ sees us. **Not** how we appear to ourselves. **Not** how we "seem" to be.

Principle #1: Forgive yourself and others.

Forgiveness is an important landmark on your journey toward wholeness. You cannot detour around it. Unforgiveness is a weighty and time-consuming distraction. Have you ever been so distracted while driving on the expressway until you missed your exit and had to drive 30 miles before the next exit? How time-consuming! That is unforgiveness. It is time-consuming. If you do not forgive yourself or others, that situation or event or deed becomes all you can dwell on. We become prisoners of that offense or act. Not only will we become distracted but even tortured by the weight of an unforgiving heart.

Matthew 18:34 states, "In anger his master turned him over to the jailers to be tortured, until he should pay back all he owed." Be released from that prison of unforgiveness. Forgive yourself and others. Do not dwell on the past. Do not dwell on that wrong exit. Get back on the highway heading in the direction of wholeness.

Principle #2: Be mindful of what you read, listen to and meditate on.

What you read, listen to and meditate on will shape your thoughts and your thoughts will influence your behavior. Philippians 4:8 (NKJV) states:

Finally, brethren, whatever things are true, whatever things are noble, whatever things are just, whatever things are pure, whatever things are lovely, whatever things are of good report, if there is any virtue and if there is anything praiseworthy – meditate on these things.

"Grasshopper thinking" will flourish only when we are meditating on negative thoughts and words. In order to put on the "Caleb-covering" we also need to associate with people who have a positive mind-set and who are encouraging and uplifting.

You will become whom you allow yourself to be influenced by. If you listen to negative and judgmental conversations day in and day out, you will find yourself talking the same way. A perfect example is small children who repeat everything they have heard. Then we want to know, where did little Susie get that!? Maybe, little Susie heard those words from you! Adults are no different. You become like your friends. I Corinthians 15:33 says, "Do not be misled: Bad company corrupts good character."

Principle #3: Know who you are.

Who are you becoming on this journey? Do you know who you are and whose you are? Take a look inward. Self-esteem is how you value yourself. Poor self-esteem mirrors condemning, negative feelings to you that cause you to think less of yourself than what God intends. Proper self-esteem is a journey of releasing the feeling that somehow you do not deserve a healthy self-esteem while others do. You must recognize and embrace that Jesus gained your self-esteem on the cross by His death and Resurrection. He paid the price for you to be all you can be. The process of comprehending God's infinite care and love for you – with unique strengths and weaknesses – puts a new light on self-esteem.

Psalm 139 expresses the wonder of being uniquely created by God. You are His. You must accept being His own. The hardest thing I have ever done on my journey toward wholeness is submitting to being the "workmanship" of God. Ephesians 2:10 (NKJV) states, "For we are His workmanship, created in Christ Jesus for good works, which God prepared beforehand that we should walk in them." I had to accept, by faith, that in my mother's womb (Psalm 139) I was created to be His workmanship (Ephesians 2:10), literally, a "masterpiece" or "a work of art" created specially for the purpose of doing good works of Him who sent me (that is, my Father, Jesus).

I am a masterpiece created to do good works which means to help others along this journey recognize who and whose they are. That is awesome! You and I are "masterpieces" created to do good works! However, the only way you and I will know what those good works are will be to submit to His will, plan and journey for our lives.

Principle #4: Believe, memorize and actualize what God's Word says about you.

In order to do those good works, you need to know what they are according to His Word. His Word is the Bible. You need to memorize and actualize and believe the words in Psalm 139:14 that, "I am fearfully and wonderfully made". You must believe that you have been custom designed and God is equipping you along this journey for specific achievements and purposes. Even your worst negative traits can be transformed into positive qualities. You must manage your life on this journey around what God says about you. Living in agreement with God's word and what it says about you can make all the difference in this world. Moving in and with God's Word will lead to strength and endurance. Moving devoid of it will lead to damaged emotions and detours along the way.

Principle #5: Understand satan's tactics and lies.

One of satan's tactics is to get us to compare ourselves to others. DON'T DO IT! Everyone is at a different point along his or her journey, so to compare where you are (or, are not) to someone else is spiritual suicide. It is so tempting to put yourself down because you are not "further ahead" (by your perception) in your journey than someone else. It states in Ecclesiastes 9:11a (AMP), " I returned and saw under the sun that the race is not to the swift nor the battle to the strong…".

Another of satan's tactics or lies is to make us think we are further along on our journey (or, more spiritually mature) than we really are. Before every trip in our car, my husband sets the odometer. When I asked him years ago, why he did that, he said, "I want to know exactly how far we have traveled". Do you know exactly how far you have traveled in Jesus? Do you know just how spiritually mature you are now? Well, one way to tell if you are maturing spiritually is to check your "fruit". John 15:2 (NKJV) states, "Every branch in Me that does not bear fruit He takes away; and every branch that bears fruit He prunes, that it may bear more fruit". My goal along life's journey is to produce good fruit – good works.

Principle #6: Appropriate "warrior thinking" not "grasshopper thinking".

In Numbers 13 verse 30 Caleb silenced the people and spoke emphatically that "we should go up and take possession of the land, for we can certainly do it." In the King James Version, it states, "we are well able"! That is warrior thinking! In and of ourselves, we can do nothing but with God, "I can do all things through Christ who strengthens me". (Philippians 4:13 NKJV)

Principle #7: Realize this is a life-long process.

Realize that this is a life-long journey to "warrior thinking" and spiritual maturity. We are becoming more and more whole and complete everyday. Everyday we must attempt to move another mile forward as expressed in Philippians 3:12-14 (NKJV): *"Not that I have already attained, or am already perfected; but I press on, that I may lay hold of that for which Christ Jesus has also laid hold of me. Brethren, I do not count myself to have apprehended; but one thing I do, forgetting those things which are behind and reaching forward to those things which are ahead, I press toward the goal for the prize of the upward call of God in Christ Jesus."*

It is not God's desire that we belittle ourselves or feel like we cannot accomplish what He has set before us: God wants us to "arrest" our "grasshopper thinking". I will never forget the time I was working on my doctorate degree and I met with my advisor. Here I was, an adult (with a masters degree), working at an excellent job, considered a leader and a woman full of confidence. Well, my advisor had spoken some very subtle "put downs" to me in our meeting. I remember driving home that day thinking, "I may not make it in this program; maybe I should quit now." I was really having a pity-party and exhibiting "grasshopper thinking". Then, God's Word started welling up in me: "CYNTHIA, YOU CAN DO ALL THINGS THROUGH CHRIST WHO

STRENGTHENS YOU!" I refused to accept satan's lies and believed God's Word! A few years later, I received my doctorate degree and shook my advisor's hand as I smiled confidently in Christ as he called me, "Dr. McGill".

Passage Five

Cautionary Course 2: Three Faces of Eve

If you find yourself committing acts that are caused by small thinking and/or low self-worth you may be a serial grasshopper thinker. Consistently thinking in this manner over a short period of time can lead to covering up who you really are and instead, pretending to be someone you are not. It is at this point that you are not at your best.

The classic motion picture "The Three Faces of Eve" is an example of a woman with multiple personalities. In "The Three Faces of Eve" actress Joanne Woodward portrays a woman with three separate personalities. Her husband believes himself to be married to a shy, dowdy, soft-spoken woman only to discover later on that there is another completely unrecognizable "face" to his wife. The second "face" is brash, loud, vulgar, and an unregenerate promiscuous woman who declares that she is not his wife nor would she even consider being his wife. Talk about confusion! In the end, with the help of a trained professional, she develops a third personality that encompasses the best parts of the first two.

There is, of course, another "Eve" with whom you are familiar. There is very little known about Eve, the first woman in the world, yet she was the final piece in the intricate and amazing puzzle of the creation. Satan, in the Garden of Eden, approached Eve where she and Adam lived. He questioned her contentment. How could she be happy when she was not allowed to eat from one of the fruit trees? With the help of satan, Eve shifted her focus from all that God had done for her and given to her to the one thing He withheld. Eve was willing to accept the viewpoint of satan without checking with God. Due to this type of thinking, she and Adam were ejected from the Garden of Eden.

When you read the story of Eve as told in Genesis 2:19-4:26, you will see that she also had three faces like the actress Joanne Woodward. The three faces are: deception, self-will and guilt. She allowed satan to **deceive** her into believing that she would die if she tasted the fruit of the Tree of Knowledge. He tried to make Eve think that sin is good, pleasant and desirable. Knowledge of both good and evil seemed harmless to her. People, like Eve, usually choose wrong things because they are deceived that those things are good, at least for themselves.

Your sins do not always appear ugly to you. Some sins may be dressed up in attractive garments such as gossip coverings that sound like, "Well, let us just pray for her because she did thus and so." So prepare yourself for the attractive deceptions that may come your way. You cannot always prevent deception, but there is always a way of escape. I Corinthians 10:13 (AMP) states: *For no temptation (no trial regarded as enticing to sin, no matter how it comes or where it leads) has overtaken you and laid hold on you that is not common to man [that is, no temptation or trial has come to you that is beyond human resistance and that is not adjusted and adapted and belonging to human experience, and such as man can bear]. But God is faithful [to His Word and to His compassionate nature], and He [can be trusted] not to let you be tempted and tried and assayed beyond your ability and strength of resistance and power to endure, but with the temptation He will [always] also provide the way out (the means of escape to a landing place), that you may be capable and strong and powerful to bear up under it patiently.*

Three points to remember when deception comes your way:

1. Wrong desires and temptations happen to everyone, so do not believe you have been singled out.
2. Others have resisted temptation, and so can you.
3. Any temptation can be resisted because God will help you resist it.

God helps you resist deception by helping you:

1. Recognize those people and situations that give you trouble.
2. Run from anything you know is wrong.
3. Choose to do only what is right.
4. Pray for the help of God.
5. Seek friends who love God and can offer help when you are attracted to deception.

Secondly, Eve became obsessed with acquiring the "wisdom" that was supposedly available to those who tasted the fruit. This caused her to place her own **"self-will"** above the will of God. God says true wisdom comes from obedience and knowing what **not** to do. The restrictions He gives you are for your good, helping you avoid the spirit of self-will. In your own self-will you can drive a car beyond the speed limit, but you do not need to hit someone or something to realize it would be foolish to do so. It was not wrong of Eve to want to "be like God". To become more like God is the highest goal of Christianity. However, satan deceived Eve concerning the right way to accomplish this goal. He told her she could become more like God by defying the authority of God, taking the place of God and imposing her own self-will concerning what was best for her life. In effect, he told her to act in her own self-will in order to become her own god. To *become like God* is not the same as trying *to become God*. To *become like God* is to reflect His characteristics and recognize His authority over your life.

Like Eve, you often have a worthy goal but try to achieve it in the wrong way. Self-will leads to rebellion against God. As soon as you begin to leave God out of your plans, you are placing yourself above Him. This is exactly what satan wants you to do.

Finally, Eve deceived Adam into tasting the fruit as well. After God ejected them both from the Garden, they were both left to suffer **guilt** and shame for their disobedience to the revealed Word of God. Their guilty feelings made them run from God and try to hide. A guilty conscience is a warning signal God placed inside you that goes off when you have done wrong. The worst step you could take is to eliminate the guilty feelings without eliminating the cause. That would be like using ibuprofen for pain but not treating the illness. Be glad those guilty feelings are there! They make you aware of your sin so you can ask for forgiveness from God and then correct your wrongdoing.

We are all unique personalities. Like "Eve", many of us exhibit multiple personalities – one for the church, one for the office, one for the people who love us and yet another for those whom we think do not love us. We wear our "goodie-goodie" faces on Sunday and the other faces during the rest of the week. God's desire is that you be whole and complete. Due to the fact that He lives and works in you, there is no need to present different faces to the world in different circumstances. The "you" that has been saved and sanctified in Christ is equal to any situation, **if** you trust God and open yourself so that He can make you whole and complete.

In order or become whole, you need to sense that you are loveable and worthy to be loved without having to qualify for that love. Children deprived of a loving relationship grow up feeling undeserving or inferior. Is that you? Are you trying to gain self-worth in all the wrong places? You need a healthy self-image that is based only on the one who created you – God.

Let God define you and shape your self-image – not the media or Internet or peers or men. What does your Creator say about His creation – **you**! Memorize the following scriptures; write them down on index cards and repeat them aloud at least twice a day for thirty days. Watch the positive difference in your attitude about yourself!

Psalm 100:3 (NIV)

Know that the Lord is God. It is He who made us, and we are His; we are His people, the sheep of His pasture.

God is your Creator; you did not create yourself. Many people live as though they are the creator and center of their own little world. This mind-set of deception leads to a greedy posses- siveness and, if everything should be taken away, a loss of hope itself. When you realize that God created you and gave you all you have, you will want to give to others as God gave to you. Then, if all is lost, you still have God and all He gives you.

Psalm 139:13-16 (NIV)

For you created my inmost being; you knit me together in my mother's womb, I praise You because I am fearfully and won- derfully made; Your works are wonderful, I know that full well. My frame was not hidden from You when I was made in the secret place. When I was woven together in the depths of the earth, Your eyes saw my unformed body. All the days ordained for me were written in Your book before one of them came to be.

The character of God goes into the creation of every per- son. When you think you are worthless or even begin to hate yourself remember that the Holy Spirit is ready and willing to work within you. God thinks of you constantly! You should have as much respect for yourself as your Maker has for you.

Jeremiah 29:11 (AMP)
For I know the thoughts and plans that I have for you, says the Lord, thoughts and plans for welfare and peace and not for evil, to give you hope in your final outcome.

God knows the future, and His plans for you are good and full of hope. As long as God who knows your future provides your agenda and goes with you as you fulfill His mission, you can have boundless hope. This does not mean you will be spared pain, suffering, or hardship, but that God will see you through to a glorious conclusion.

II Corinthians 5:17 (AMP)
Therefore if any person is [ingrafted] in Christ (the Messiah) he is a new creation (a new creature altogether); the old [previous moral and spiritual condition] has passed away. Behold, the fresh and new has come!

Christians are brand new people on the *inside*. The Holy Spirit gives them new life, and they are not the same anymore. You are not reformed, rehabilitated or reeducated – you are recreated, living in vital union with Christ. You are not merely turning over a new leaf; you are beginning a new life under a new Master.

You should now see a positive difference in your attitude about yourself. By memorizing these scriptures you will stop pretending to be someone you are not and begin respecting yourself as the woman of excellence on the inside that shines forth on the outside.

Make it a practice to keep your light "trimmed and burning"; clear of deception, self-will and guilt. These faces can cause great tribulation for yourself as well as others. Replace these faces with the Word of God so that you can have the best view of the road on your way to Living Whole Highway!

Passage Six

Cautionary Course 3: Stop Entertaining Those Unforgiving Thoughts!

Don't you see that stop sign? Do you know what that sign is telling you to do? It is telling you to come to a **FULL STOP**; go, when it is safe! Well, when will it be safe? It will be safe once you take the time to understand what unforgiving thoughts can do to you.

Read Matthew 18:21-35. In this scripture, Jesus tells the parable of the unforgiving debtor. It begins with Peter asking Jesus if seven was enough times to forgive someone. Jesus answered, "Seventy-seven times", meaning that we should not even entertain how many times we forgive someone. The scripture continues on to discuss the unforgiving debtor. The master in this story represents God. The servant represents us. We owed a huge debt to God (the master) but God cancelled our debt. He forgave our sins. Then, the first chance we (the servant) gets to forgive someone else (another servant), we do not want to forgive the debt. How soon we forget! God (the master) forgave us and let us go but we do not want to forgive anyone.

Well, have you really looked at the consequences of unforgiveness? If you do not forgive, your Heavenly Father will turn us over to the jailers **to be tortured** – How are you tortured? You are tortured by…

❖ Migraine headaches
❖ Ulcers and other illnesses
❖ Delusions and living in a fantasy world
❖ Depression
❖ Poverty

If you *do not forgive*, God will turn you over to be tortured. I can hear you saying…

"He hurt me."

"She lied on me."

"They talked about me."

"I am supposed to forgive him/her and release them?"

"I am the one who took her to lunch".

"I gave him the best years of my life".

"I befriended them when everyone warned me that they are dishonest."

"I am the one that was good to her, but she lied on me."

"Now, I am supposed to forgive him/her/them?!?"

Others may even be dealing with deeper issues of unforgiveness…

*"Dr. McGill, you do not understand. I can forgive the one who gossiped about me and caused me great grief. But I am supposed to forgive that man who raped me? I am supposed to forgive my husband who broke my heart and lied to me? I am supposed to forgive the father/mother who left me? Why must I be the one who forgives? After all, I am the one who was hurt, harmed and devastated. Again I ask, **WHY** must I be the one who forgives?"*

BECAUSE CHRIST FORGAVE FIRST.

Isaiah 53:5 (AMP) states, "But He was wounded for our transgressions, He was bruised for our guilt and iniquities; the chastisement [needful to obtain] peace and well-being for us was upon Him, and with the stripes [that wounded] Him we are healed and made whole."

Luke 23:34 (AMP) states, "And Jesus prayed, Father, forgive them, for they know not what they do. And they divided His garments and distributed them by casting lots for them."

Jesus asked God to forgive the people who were putting Him to death – Jewish leaders, Roman politicians and soldiers, bystanders – and God answered that prayer by opening up the way of salvation even to the murderers of Jesus. If you are to be Christ-like – you must forgive.

Forgive means to release and untie. If you do not let offenders off your hook, you are hooked to them and the past. Why do I say, "Hooked"? Simply put, it means that the offender is all you reflect on morning, noon and night. He or she stays on your mind and what was done to you. That just means continued pain for you. **STOP THE PAIN! LET IT GO!** You do not forgive someone merely for his or her sake. You do it for your sake so **YOU CAN BE FREE**. Free from migraines, ulcers, other illnesses, delusions, depression, etc. Matthew 18:35 (AMP) states, "So also My heavenly Father will deal with every one of you if you do not freely forgive your brother from your heart his offenses." Since God has forgiven all your sins, you should not withhold forgiveness from others. Realizing how completely Christ has forgiven you should produce a free and generous attitude of forgiveness toward others.

Forgiveness must be from the heart and not the head. Your only choice is whether you will do so in the **bondage of bitterness** or the **freedom from forgiveness**. If you do not forgive, bitterness will imprison you. How do you forgive from the heart? First, you acknowledge **the hurt** and **the hate**. If your forgiveness does not visit the emotional core of your past, it will be incomplete. This is what I call the "Great Christian Cover-up". Christians feel the pain of interpersonal offenses, but we will not acknowledge them. Let God bring the pain to the surface so He can deal with it. This is when and where the healing takes place. You have truly forgiven when you no longer feel the pain when you see the person or think of the incident.

Is there someone you have never forgiven? They are hooked to you. Write their name and state what they did to you. State what it is doing to you emotionally, physically and spiritually. Forgiveness is a process of recognizing a transgression done to you by another person, feeling the emotional pain and then deciding to let go of the anger and bitterness thus receiving the grace of God. His power and His healing consequently clear up all the murkiness, static and the obstructions between Jesus and you.

Forgiveness is surgery on the Tumor of Resentment. The reason many are in poor health is because they have tumors of resentment. They believe they have forgiven but they really have not forgiven. That is why you may still have anger and resentment. Forgiveness is surgery on the tumor. Have you heard of people that go to the medical doctor and are told that physically nothing can be found wrong with them, but psychologically they are a wreck! Plus, if the medical doctor is not a Christian, they do not know Jesus so they give you medicine for depression. Essentially, you are suffering from not being able to forgive. Being unable to forgive can cause one to experience migraine headaches. Cancer has never run in you family but all of a sudden you have a cancerous growth. At times disease is a generational curse but some infirmities are due to not being able to forgive.

Do you know why some people can be "on cloud nine"? It is because they have chosen to forgive. If you do not forgive, you will clog yourself up. Think about how you feel when you cannot go to the bathroom. Weigh that natural clog up with a spiritual clog up. Forgiveness is your fiber. Being clogged is a very bad feeling. When you are clogged you have no joyfulness and you are miserable and no one wants to be around you. You cannot say anything to them…you are depressed. If you want to stay spiritually clogged up then you will be bogged down with the inability to be able to forgive. You cannot pray; you cannot even jump for joy.

Now let me tell you some erroneous beliefs of why you do not forgive. One is, "I forgave them once and it did not work". Forgiving someone is a process. Why do you think the Bible said, "Forgive seventy times"? This means you may have to come back to the altar 100 times. It is OK!

Like the onion theory, when you pull back the layer of the onion and remove one layer, how many more do you have – a bunch! Some have been wounded so many times as children that they have a whole bunch of layers to pull back. Being hurt by fathers, mothers, sisters, and brothers and even people in the church (and they are suppose to be Christians) causes profound injury. It is an onion and you may have to keep peeling. Repeat the process.

An additional mistaken belief is, "I do not feel like forgiving". It is a choice ladies, not a feeling. Some days I do not feel like I am saved but I am. It is not a feeling; it is a choice. Do you want this hanging on for the rest of your life? It is a choice not a feeling.

An added stumbling block is when you say, "If I forgive them I am saying the act is OK". I tell the ladies at New Life Fellowship, "I do not care if you came out butt naked and sat on his lap – your father, uncle, grandfather did not have the right to hurt you. There are limitations, which means if your uncle raped you, you do not take your baby over to him to baby-sit just because you have forgiven him".

Refuse to be tortured. In Matthew it says if you do not forgive you will be tortured. Let me share something with you. There was someone who hurt me real bad. I thought I was going to help her but instead she hurt me. I had to forgive her about 50 times for months. I had to forgive her because I was trying to get to heaven and I do not want to be clogged.

Since God has forgiven them by His grace, you can forgive them too.

For each person on your list, say:

"Lord, I choose this day to forgive (List Names) for (tell Jesus what they did to you). Jesus I release them right now. Lord, by faith I am doing this because you have forgiven me and I am to forgive others. And Lord I no longer want to be tortured. I no longer want those offenses to define who I am. Lord I have positive self-esteem. You, Jesus, affirm me. I am fearfully and wonderfully made and I am not junk because you do not make any junk! I am worthy of your love, Lord. I am worthy to be loved by others, Lord and worthy to love myself. Therefore, I forgive (List Names) by faith in the name of Jesus".

Keep praying about each individual until you are sure that all the remembered pain is gone. Do not rationalize or explain the behavior of the offender. Forgiveness deals with your pain, not the behavior of another. If you are tired of being stopped up and you have decided you want to experience the freedom of the Holy Spirit then you are all set to tear up the pages you finished and put them in the garbage. It is a choice; tear it up as a symbol of freedom, in the name of Jesus.

Now that you are free, it is safe for you to go!

Passage Seven

He Has Done It All

If you have successfully crossed over the cautionary courses and accessed freedom from grasshopper thinking, deception, self-will, guilt and unforgiveness, you are now on the road of reassurance that God has done it all for you! In this reassurance are things you will have to work at to continue to get your breakthrough. What are some of the ways in which you can get your breakthrough?

HE HAS DONE IT ALL! PRAISE HIM!

Psalm 9:1-2 (AMP) states,

I will praise You, O Lord, with my whole heart; I will show forth (recount and tell aloud) all Your marvelous works and wonderful deeds! I will rejoice in You and be in high spirits; I will sing praise to Your name, O Most High!

Praise is expressing to God your appreciation and understanding of His worth. It is saying "thank you" for each aspect of His divine nature. Your inward attitude becomes outward expression. When you praise God, you help yourself by expanding your awareness of WHO HE IS!

BE OBEDIENT AND LISTEN! HE HAS DONE IT ALL!

In Joshua 6 the walls of Jericho fall. It must have been strange to the Israelites that, instead of going to battle, they were going to march around the city for a week! This was the plan of God, and the Israelites had a guaranteed victory if they would follow it. As strange as the plan sounded, it worked.

The instructions of God may require you to travel a way that does not make sense at first. Even as you follow Him, you may wonder how things can possibly work out. Like the Israelites, take one day at a time and follow step by step. You may not see the logic behind the plan of God until after you have obeyed.

HE HAS DONE IT ALL! STUDY AND ACT ON THE WORD!

The Bible can sit on your bookshelf and gather dust, or you can make it a vital part of your life by regularly setting aside time to study. When you discover the wisdom of the message of God, you will want to apply it to your life and pass it on to your family and others. Your family and others will see the passion you have for studying the Word of God and recognize that the Bible is not merely good reading – it is real help for real life.

HE HAS DONE IT ALL! PRAY!

Psalm 5:1-3 (AMP) states,

Listen to my words, O Lord, give heed to my sighing and groaning. Hear the sound of my cry, my King and my God, for to You do I pray. In the morning You hear my voice, O Lord; in the morning I prepare [a prayer, a sacrifice] for You and watch and wait [for You to speak to my heart].

The secret of breakthrough is having a close relationship with God. The secret of a close relationship with God is to pray to Him earnestly each morning. In the morning your mind is free from problems and then you can commit the whole day to God. Regular prayer helps develop an intimate friendship with God and is certainly necessary for a strong relationship with God.

You need to communicate with Him daily. Do you have a regular time to pray and read the Word of God?

There is one more word – **BELIEVE!** If you do not believe, all that praying, reading, etc. is ineffective.

Before you can pass over to the last 3 passages we need to cover 3 areas that are needed in order to get your breakthrough to becoming a woman of grace, faith, excellence and virtue. The three areas are:

❖ **INTIMACY WITH GOD**
❖ **POSITIVE SELF-ESTEEM**
❖ **GODLY INTIMACY WITH OTHERS**

Your breakthrough will come in a different way for you than it may come for others but there needs to be a Godly balance in all three areas of your life.

INTIMACY WITH GOD

Intimacy with God is mentioned first because you have to have an intimate relationship with God in order to know who God says you are (self-esteem). Intimacy with God starts with studying and acting on His Word. You have to study. Attending Sunday service and midweek Bible study is not enough to become intimate with God. The only way you are going to know if God loves you is to spend time with Him. Not just petitioning Him, always "gimme, gimme", but listening to Him and letting Him love you.

God and Moses are a wonderful example of "intimacy with God". Moses and God talked back and forth with each other, just as friends do. Why did Moses find such favor with God? It certainly was not because he was gifted, perfect or powerful. Rather, it was because God chose Moses, and Moses in turn relied wholeheartedly on the wisdom and direction of God. Friendship with God was a true privilege for Moses, out of reach for the other Hebrews. However, it is not out of reach for you today. Jesus called His disciples, all of His followers, His friends. He has called you to be His friend. Will you trust Him as Moses did?

POSITIVE SELF-ESTEEM

If you are continually praying but not acting on what God has told you, and not believing who you are in Christ, then you could still end up with a poor self-esteem. I have observed lots of prayer warriors who do not love themselves. After they pray they do not love other people either. Do you know someone like that or am I describing you?

GODLY INTIMACY WITH OTHERS

If you do not love yourself you cannot love others. God wants us to love our sisters and brothers. Naomi and Ruth are beautiful examples of "Godly intimacy with others". Their ages, cultures and family backgrounds were very different. As mother-in-law and daughter-in-law, they probably had as many opportunities for tension as they did for tenderness. Yet, they were bound in Godly intimacy to each other. They shared great affection for each other, deep sorrow and an overriding commitment to God. Yet, as much as they depended on each other, they also gave each other freedom in their commitment to one another. Naomi was willing to let Ruth return to her family. Ruth was willing to leave her homeland to go to Israel. God was at the center of their intimate communication. Ruth came to know God through Naomi. The older woman allowed Ruth to feel, hear and see all the anguish and joy of her relationship with God.

How often do you feel that your questions and thoughts about God should be left out of a close relationship? How often do you share your unedited thoughts about God with your friends or spouse? Sharing openly about your relationship with God can bring depth and intimacy to your relationships with others.

The relationship Ruth and Naomi shared was strengthened because their greatest bond was faith in God. It was also strengthened because of their strong mutual commitment and each woman tried to do what was best for the other. The lesson to be learned from their lives is that the living presence of God in a relationship overcomes differences that might otherwise create disharmony and division.

God has done it all for you!
When you praise Him,
He expands your awareness of who He is!
When you are obedient and listen,
the walls in your life will fall!
When you study and act on the Word, He shows you wisdom!

When you pray, He will communicate with you!

When you believe, He will strengthen you!

When you have intimacy with God, a positive self-esteem and intimacy with others, you are on your way to discovering without a shadow of a doubt, that…

God loves you,

you are accepted by Him and

HE HAS DONE IT ALL!

Now you MAKE THE DECLARATION…

God has done it all for ME!

When I praise Him, He expands MY awareness of who He is!

When I AM obedient and listen, the walls in MY life will fall!

When I study and act on the Word, He shows ME wisdom!

When I pray, He will communicate with ME!

When I believe, He will strengthen ME!

When I have intimacy with God, a positive self-esteem and intimacy with others,

I AM on MY way to discovering without a shadow of a doubt, that…

God loves ME,

I AM accepted by Him and

HE HAS DONE IT ALL!

Passage Eight

I Know That Full Well

Thus far you have traveled a journey that has helped you fully comprehend and understand the breadth, length, height and depth of the devotion and love God has towards you. You have survived the cautionary passages that concluded with a light at the end of the tunnel that shown forth the reassurance that God had done it all for you.

Now this part of the journey will provide you with a few basic truths that will allow you to "know that you know that you know" you are well connected and whole. This passage will give you insight and knowledge that will prepare you for the final "inner change" on to "Living Whole Highway".

Let's begin by reading Genesis 1:26-27 (AMP)…

God said, Let Us [Father, Son and Holy Spirit] make mankind in Our image, after Our likeness, and let them have complete authority over the fish of the sea, the birds of the air, the [tame] beasts, and over all of the earth, and over everything that creeps upon the earth. So God created man in His own image, in the image and likeness of God He created him; male and female He created them.

Knowing that you are made in the image of God and thus share many of His characteristics provides a solid basis for the declaration "I KNOW THAT FULL WELL". This declaration is not defined by achievements, physical attractiveness, possessions or public acclaim. Instead, the declaration comes from knowing that you are made in the image of God.

Knowing that you are a person of infinite worth gives you the freedom to love God (Intimacy with God), know who you are in Christ (Self-esteem), and make a valuable contribution to those around you (Godly Intimacy with Others).

When I view and consider Your heavens, the work of Your fingers, the moon and the stars, which You have ordained and established, what is man that You are mindful of him, and the son of [earthborn] man that you care for him? Yet you have made him but a little lower than God [or heavenly beings], and You have crowned him with glory and honor. Psalm 8:3-5 (AMP)

God created you only a little lower than the angels! Remember "FULL WELL" that God considers you highly valuable. You have great worth because you bear the stamp of the Creator (remember Genesis 1:26 & 27?). Traveling this road to Living Whole Highway should have enlightened you to the facts that Christ has begun and is beginning His work in you. On this journey your progress has been in His able care. You set a goal and put all your energies toward moving forward in Christ in order to fulfill your destiny and enjoy the promises of God. You have followed the directions of the Holy Spirit who has led you on this journey.

The Holy Spirit, your Peace Officer, similar to a traffic officer, has motioned for you to stop at the world's green lights and signaled you to drive through the world's red lights and stop signs in order to get to this point in your journey. The world and those of the world do not understand the journey you are on. It is not for them to understand...

It is better to trust and take refuge in the Lord than to put confidence in man. Psalm 118:8 (AMP)

Each day you must put your confidence in and trust God, Jesus and the Holy Spirit (Peace Officer) to guide you through this world in order to reach and reside on Living Whole Highway.

Know that you are up to the very edge of the Promised Land. He, (the Peace Officer) has protected you and fulfilled every promise. He is encouraging you to travel the last few miles of faith in order to enter Living Whole Highway. He has brought you this far – He will not let you down now.

Let's look at what the Peace Officer needs you to know FULL WELL as you travel these last few miles:

FULL
Phillippians 1:6
WELL

And I am convinced and sure of this very thing, that He who began a good work in you will continue until the day of Jesus Christ [right up to the time of His return], developing [that good work] and perfecting and bringing it to full completion in you. (AMP)

God, who begins His good work in you will continue it throughout your life and will finish it. Be assured (I KNOW FULL WELL!) that your progress is in His able care. When God starts a project,

He finishes it! God will help you grow in grace until He has completed His work in your life. He promises to finish the work He has begun. Remember His promise and provision.

Accordingly God also, in His desire to show more convincingly and beyond doubt to those who were to inherit the promise the unchangeableness of His purpose and plan, intervened (mediated) with an oath. This was so that, by two unchangeable things [His promise and His oath] in which it is impossible for God ever to prove false or deceive us, we who have fled [to Him] for refuge might have mighty indwelling strength and strong encouragement to grasp and hold fast the hope appointed for us and set before [us]. [Now] we have this [hope] as a sure and steadfast anchor of the soul [it cannot slip and it cannot break down under whoever steps out upon it – a hope] that reaches farther and enters into [the very certainty of the Presence] within the veil... (AMP)

There are two unchangeable realities about God: His nature and His promise. God embodies all truth, and therefore He cannot lie. So, with God being truth, you can be secure in His promises. God gives an unconditional promise of acceptance.

And God saw everything that He had made, and behold, it was very good (suitable, pleasant) and He approved it completely... (AMP)

God is pleased with how He made you! You are valuable to Him! Enough said! I KNOW THAT FULL WELL!

But you are a chosen race, a royal priesthood, a dedicated nation, [God's] own purchased, special people, that you may set forth the wonderful deeds and display the virtues and perfections of Him Who called you out of darkness into His marvelous light. Once you were not a people [at all], but now you are God's people; once you were unpitied; but now you are pitied and have received mercy. (AMP)

Your relationship with Jesus Christ is far more important than jobs, knowledge, success or wealth. God has chosen you as His very own. Remember (I KNOW THAT FULL WELL!) that your value comes from being one of His children, not from what you can achieve. You have worth because of what God does, not because of what you do.

But He said to me, my grace (My favor and lovingkindness and mercy) is enough for you [sufficient against any danger and enables you to bear the trouble manfully]; for My strength and power are made perfect (fulfilled and completed) and show themselves most effective in [your] weakness. Therefore, I will all the more gladly glory in my weaknesses and infirmities, that the strength and power of Christ (the Messiah) may rest (yes, may pitch a tent over and dwell) upon me! So for the sake of Christ, I am well pleased and take pleasure in infirmities, insults, hardships, persecutions, perplexities and distresses; for when I am weak [in human strength], then am I [truly] strong (able, powerful in divine strength). (AMP)

You must rely on God for your effectiveness. When you are weak, allowing God to fill you with His power, then you are stronger than you could ever be on your own. When hindrances and setbacks come (which they will), you must depend on God. Only His power makes you effective for Him and helps you do work that has lasting value.

For you did form my inward parts; You did knit me together in my mother's womb. I will confess and praise You for You are fearful and wonderful and for the awful wonder of my birth! Wonderful are your works, and that my inner self knows right well. My frame was not hidden from you when I was being formed in secret [and] intricately and curiously wrought [as if embroidered with various colors] in the depths of the earth [a region of darkness and mystery]. Your eyes say my unformed substance and in Your book all the days [of my life] were written before ever they took shape, when as yet there was none of them. (AMP)

Your journey to wholeness will start to take shape when YOU KNOW FULL WELL, not just in your mind but also in your heart, the true meaning of this scripture. You must first acknowledge and understand (KNOW FULL WELL) that God and God alone created you – not Allah, not Buddha — God. Not a cosmic explosion, not "a higher power" — God. This is an extremely crucial mile marker to pass on your journey. Only God formed you in the womb of your mother. The last phrase in verse 14 reads: "Wonderful are Your works, and that my inner self knows right well". Remember the bumper sticker on some vehicles: "God doesn't make junk"? Well, you **are not** junk! You are not an accident, an insignificant human being, nor a mistake simply here to occupy space and pay taxes! The works of God are awesome, therefore you are one of His special and unique "works" which makes you AWESOME! Look in the (in)side view mirror of your vehicle! Gaze upon one of God's breathtaking wonders; a wonder as beautiful as a rose garden or as magnificent as a rainbow. The awesome sight you see should cause you to whisper, "Yes, the works of God are wonderful and I KNOW THAT FULL WELL."

My progress is in His able care!
I am secure in His promises!
God is pleased with how He made me!
God has chosen me as His very own!
His power makes me effective for Him and
helps me do work that has lasting value!
I KNOW THIS FULL WELL!

The Journey To Wholeness

Passage Nine

Well-Connected

An important part of being whole is being well-connected to other women. Do you have wholesome, healthy friendships with other women? Do you have some friendships that may even be considered "toxic"? Is it difficult for you to make lasting, healthy friendships with other women your age? If you have no healthy female friendships, do you know why?

I certainly do not mean to be crude or insensitive but we women can be petty and a bit (well, sometimes, a whole lot) jealous of each other. Why? Maybe, we do not love ourselves as we should. We must certainly love ourselves before we can love others. Also, we must possess a sense of security and a positive self-esteem in order to promote and embrace a healthy female friendship.

Sometimes, friendships can be toxic – destroying your sense of self-worth. Webster's New World Dictionary defines toxic as poisonous. Carefully consider whether any of your relationships with women are "poisonous". Of course, we could include relationships with men in this discussion; however, I would like us to focus on our "girlfriends" for now.

Does your girlfriend constantly berate you? Are most of your discussions with her centered on "putting down" other people? Do you or she want your friendship to be exclusive of other women? Do you want to consume the other's time day in and day out? Face it; your relationship is TOXIC – POISONOUS.

God desires that you have friends but He wants them to be healthy relationships. Sometimes you cannot grow beyond your friends and if you do, a feud begins. However, it is possible to outgrow your girlfriend. If you are maturing on this journey and your friend is not, you may need to reexamine that friendship.

I Corinthians 15:33 (NIV) states that you should "not be misled, bad company corrupts good character". Oftentimes we think to ourselves, "Oh, I will be a good influence on that person. She needs me". Do not be deceived! If your friend's tongue and/ or behavior are toxic, you **will** be affected.

There came a time I had to reevaluate my freindships. I soon came to realize that no matter how hard I tried not to let their negativity affect me, it did! I cannot be around someone who negatively judges others through an entire conversation. Negativity will poison your system. God desires that you elevate your mind, your thoughts, your speech and your heart on positive, uplifting conversation and deeds.

In Philippians 4:8 (NIV), Jesus instructs us: "Finally, brothers, whatever is true, whatever is noble, whatever is right, whatever is pure, whatever is lovely, whatever is admirable – if anything is excellent or praiseworthy – think about such things."

I have had to put some distance between some long time friends and me because of their negativity. I had to realize that Jesus wants to sanctify all of me as well as all of my relationships. Jesus wants me to be "well-connected"; connected in healthy relationships with other women. Positive relationships that are not spent judging and condemning others.

Are you well-connected or in poisonous relationships with other women? Along this journey, at a critical juncture, you will need to reexamine your relationships and ask God if these relationships are pleasing in His sight. At this mile of my journey, I want to truly please God in every area of my life. Some of those toxic friendships were weighing me and my luggage down and I had to make a decision as to whether I was going to sustain unhealthy relationships or not.

Seek God and He will direct you to healthy female friendships. How do you sustain healthy relationships? Well, in order to have a healthy relationship, you must be healthy. And, by that I mean, you must not thrive on and seek gossip. You cannot be judgmental and critical. You cannot let your conversation be consumed with putting others down.

Are you positive and encouraging? Are your behaviors fruitful to a healthy friendship? Are you a good friend to have? Are you giving and nurturing? Do you forgive? Do you keep confidences? Once you search yourself and determine what you can contribute to a relationship, then you can seek the same attributes in a friend.

Search yourself before searching for a friend. Ask God for a Naomi-Ruth or David-Jonathan kind of friendship.

Friendships that are healthy, nurturing, and will last a lifetime.

Passage Ten

Living Whole Highway

You made it thus far! Congratulations! What a journey! Needless to say, the journey continues (as long as you are living) however, you are probably traveling with a lot less baggage and taking fewer detours. So, how do we stay on the Living Whole Highway?

One thing I know: I want to be real. I want to be real in dealing with my husband, my children, with other women, and most of all, with God! I do not just want to say or do what I think others want. I no longer want to play games. Take me as I am. So, the very first way to live whole is to be real — be you; not who you think others want you to be.

I have always struggled with the impossible weight of perfectionism. Not only did I expect myself to be perfect and do everything exactly right, I would expect everyone around me to be perfect. I have learned throughout the years on this journey that Jesus is not asking for perfection. He is asking for broken people who want to be filled with more of Him, not perfect people full of some unattainable illusions of perfection.

Gail Sheehy wrote a classic work on women's issues entitled **<u>Passages: Predictable Crises of Adult Life.</u>**[1] In it she writes, "With each passage (or transition from one stage to another in life) some magic must be given up, some cherished illusion of safety and comfortably familiar sense of self must be cast off to allow for the greater expansion of our own distinctiveness."[1]

Another treasure I discovered along the way is that self-esteem is something to be discovered within you. You cannot look at outward trappings – jobs, children, husbands, homes, and social status – to define your self-esteem. Self-esteem is a God given gift; for you are His "workmanship" (Ephesians 2:10). You are "fearfully and wonderfully made" (Psalm 139:13-16). You have a "purpose" and a "destiny" (Ephesians 1:11 NIV). God affirms you. You have His seal of approval. Therefore, people can only reaffirm you. You can only restate what God has already asserted to be true. Only God can state that I am a "new creature" (II Corinthians 5:17 NIV) and part of a "royal priesthood" (I Peter 2:9) and no longer living "under condemnation" (Romans 8:1 NIV) and that my "price is far above rubies" (Proverbs 31:10 NIV).

My Creator is the only one who I should look to for affirmation; for the truth about who I am. When I look to God for affirmation, I do not stumble on this journey when someone does not reaffirm me or wants me to live up to their expectations rather than God's.

The Word of God affirms me and makes me whole. Webster defines "whole" as "in sound health; not defective; entire, complete; in all aspects of one's being, including physical,

---

[1]Gail Sheeby, Passages: Predictable Crises of Adult Life, (New York:Bantam, 1976) pg. 31.

mental, social, etc." I am learning that in order to maintain wholeness, my spirit, soul and body must be whole and in balance. When my body is in pain, it seems that my soul and spirit are in pain as well.

Sometimes as women, we must give up, it seems, part of ourselves for others. It felt like I had given up part of myself in order to have a harmonious marriage. It seemed as if I had given up some "of me" in order to be a good mother. The conclusion I have come to is: Yes, I have given up the selfish parts of me and my desires and dreams. Due to my desire to be a good wife, mother, friend and woman I have allowed God to work on me to become less selfish and more others-oriented. So, in actuality, I have only given up what God wants me to release anyway.

The journey for me began the moment I died to self and said, "Lord, have your way in my life." Then, and only then, did Jesus begin to show me obstacles to becoming whole and fulfilled. It is so easy to go along in life thinking you have it altogether and that everyone else is off course. However, when you stop and shine the light on yourself, then and only then do you realize that some adjustments to your own course must be made, if you want to become a whole, complete, mature woman.

I must maintain a balance. Just like I feed my body, I must feed my spirit. I must feed my spirit the truths of God. I am learning that God wants me to pack His truths in my heart. So, I am packing:

❖ **Desire** – a desire to see others reach their full potential.
❖ **Acceptance** – Learning to accept others as well as my self.

❖ **Trust** – Trust others again even when I have been hurt, lied on and falsely accused.

❖ **Diversity** – Surrounding myself with a diverse group of people – diverse in culture, race, thought and personalities.

❖ **Words** – Understanding more and more each day that the words I speak have the power to bless or curse my family, others and myself. I must learn to use words wisely.

❖ **Passion** – I must fulfill my passion! I must be passionate about what God is passionate about; God wants women whole and therefore so do I! That is why passion is an important truth to pack.

God is still working on me because becoming whole and complete is an ever-evolving process. The further I go on my journey, the further I realize that I need to adjust and move out. But, with God I know I can stay the course on the "Living Whole Highway".

My prayer is that after reading this book you now can say that your goal is to know Christ, to be like Christ and to be all Christ has in mind for you. May this one goal absorb all your energy! Do not let anything take your eyes off the road called Living Whole Highway for this is the road that leads you to know Christ in His fullness.

Forget all that you left behind when you began reading this book. We have all done things for which we are ashamed…do not live in the tension of what you have been and what you want to be. Living with such tension is like standing in the middle of a highway trying to dodge traffic coming from both directions. Your hope is now in Christ, so let go of past guilt, stay on Living Whole Highway and push forward to what God would have you to become. Grow in the knowledge of God by concentrating on your relationship with Him now. Realize that you are forgiven, and then move on to a life of faith and obedience. Look forward to a fuller and more meaningful life because of your hope in Christ.

I would like to pass on to you one last set of directions. Continuing on Living Whole Highway means remaining in Christ. The five guidelines to remaining in Christ are:

1. Accepting as truth that Christ is the Son of God.

Anyone who confesses (acknowledges, owns) that Jesus is the Son of God, God abides (lives, makes His home) in him and he [abides, lives, makes his home] in God. I John 4:15 AMP

2. Receiving Him as Redeemer and Lord.

But to as many as did receive and welcome Him, He gave the authority (power, privilege, right) to become the children of God, that is, to those who believe in (adhere to, trust in, and rely on) His name. John 1:12 AMP

3. Doing what God speaks.

All who keep His commandments [who obey His orders and follow His plan, live and continue to live, to stay and] abide in Him, and He in them. [They let Christ be a home to them and they are the home of Christ.] And by this we know and understand and have the proof that He [really] lives and makes His home in us; by the [Holy] Spirit Whom He has given us. I John 3:24 AMP

4. Continuing to have faith in the gospel.

As for you, keep in your hearts what you have heard from the beginning. If what you heard from the first dwells and remains in you, then you will dwell in the Son and in the Father [always]. I John 2:24 AMP

5.   Linking in love to the body of Christ.

This is my commandment: that you love one another [just] as I have loved you. John 15:12 AMP

A lot of folks try to be decent, honest people who do what is right. However, Jesus says that the only way to live a truly good life is to stay close to Him. Apart from Christ our hard work is like trying to operate a car when the gas tank is empty – you are not going anywhere! When the gas tank is on "F" – FULL, FAITHFUL, FAVOR, FELLOWSHIP, FILLED, FIRM, FIRST, FIXED, FORGIVING, FREE, FULFILLED – God is glorified!

You have now been set free from the consequences of sin, from self-deception, and from deception by satan. Go forth in this freedom as Jesus himself clearly shows you the way to eternal life with God on Living Whole Highway!

4-6-02
8/20 Faith By Line

13th 4-26 + 27
Go Thru But dont stay 420
Hb 11:6, 11

ABOUT THE AUTHOR

Dr. Cynthia L. McGill is the Founder and CEO of *Price-less Vessels,* ™ *Inc.* a national organization designed for senior-level executive women who desire to be empowered and become whole in character, spirit, purpose and destiny. In addition she serves as the Co-Pastor and Chief Administrative Officer of New Life Fellowship in Rochester, New York. Dr. McGill is also the Founder and President of *Women of Excellence Ministries*, a ministry of New Life Fellowship which focuses on all women of all ages, from all pathways of life and from all races and cultures.

"I believe women have immeasurable authority to influence their family, friends and society. Therefore I am called to speak passionately to women about every situation in their lives with compassion and honesty."

Thus Dr. Cynthia L. McGill sums up her purpose and passion. Many women have been defrauded or cheated themselves of joyous living by their ignorance of their spiritual make-up and their need to accept their position. Dr. McGill believes women have immeasurable authority to impact their households, friends and society. She talks passionately to women addressing every situation in their lives with tenderness, honesty and practicality. Her questions are challenging and her counsel specific.

Dr. Cynthia L. McGill is a distinguished speaker, consultant and popular retreat and seminar lecturer who purposes to assist women so that they will use their unique talents, backgrounds and experiences to become effective leaders. She focuses principally in 3 spheres: personal growth and development, win-win relationships and spiritual growth. She integrates a wealth of sound Bible truths with her individual experiences in a passionate style that presents women with a pathway that leads these "Priceless

Vessels ™ " toward their purpose. Hundreds of women from all over the nation have been delivered and transformed at her lectures and workshops.

Dr. McGill studied at the University of Rochester where she was conferred with a Bachelor of Arts in English. She gained a Master of Science degree in Instructional Technology from Rochester Institute of Technology. She crowned her educational pursuits with a Doctor of Philosophy degree in Higher Education Administration from the State University of New York at Buffalo.

Dr. McGill was Assistant Provost at Rochester Institute of Technology for six years and an administrator of several programs at RIT and other universities during her twenty (20) year secular career. Dr. McGill has been mentoring young women for many years in her church, the Greater Rochester community and while employed at RIT. During her service at RIT, she mentored many women into leadership positions. When she was promoted to Assistant Provost she was invited by the Provost to assume an Institute-wide role in evaluating mentoring programs available to all students throughout RIT. In the course of this undertaking she provided several recommendations that led to improvements at this institute of higher learning.

Dr. McGill has been inducted into the Phi Kappa Phi Honor Society and was elected (1 of 100 women) a member of the esteemed "Leadership America 1991," a national project organized by the Foundation of Women's Resources. She also received the honor of being named as a member of Outstanding Women of America in 1982.

Within New Life Fellowship, Dr. McGill has established a Leadership Training Institute that trains members of the congregation to take on leadership roles within the church as well as within the community. This Training Institute has become a model for other churches across the nation who ask for advice and instruction from Dr. McGill. She has established annual women's conferences in the Greater Rochester community for several years and instituted monthly fellowships for women within her church home. She has recently created "High Teas" with women from our community, which is an elegant celebration of women and their accomplishments.

Dr. McGill's husband, Rev. Reginald A. McGill is the Founder and Senior Pastor of New Life Fellowship. Together they are a dynamic, engaging, insightful, and God loving union who are commissioned to address the challenges that face all races and cultures. Cynthia and Reginald have two daughters, Maia and Adrienne McGill and one granddaughter, Gabrielle.